Teddy Bears
IN CROSS STITCH

Julie Hasler

MEREHURST

The projects in this book were all stitched with DMC stranded cotton embroidery threads. The keys given with each chart also list thread combinations for those who wish to use Anchor or Madeira threads. It should be pointed out that the shades produced by different companies vary slightly, and it is not always possible to find identical colours in a different range.

Published in 1993 by Merehurst Limited
Ferry House, 51-57 Lacy Road, Putney, London SW15 1PR
Text & charts copyright © Julie Hasler
Photography & illustrations copyright © 1993 Merehurst Limited
ISBN 1 85391 226 3
Reprinted 1993, 1994, 1995 (Twice), 1996, 1999

A catalogue record for this book is available from the British Library.

Managing Editor Heather Dewhurst
Edited by Diana Brinton
Designed by Maggie Aldred
Photography by Debbie Patterson
Illustrations by John Hutchinson
Typesetting by BMD Graphics, Hemel Hempstead
Colour separation by Fotographics Limited, UK – Hong Kong
Printed in Hong Kong by Wing King Tong

Merehurst is the leading publisher of craft books and has an excellent range of titles to suit all levels. Please send to the address above for our free catalogue, stating the title of this book.

CONTENTS

INTRODUCTION

The favourite stitch of our great-grandmothers, and found in folk art the world over, cross stitch is becoming increasingly popular these days for the decoration of household furnishings, linen and children's clothes. The teddy bear is a much more recent invention, being named after America's 26th president, Theodore Roosevelt. In this book, these two popular themes are happily united, to offer a range of attractive and amusing projects.

Some designs, such as the greetings cards or the trinket box lids, are small, and will prove quick to embroider and so simple that they would make an ideal introduction to cross stitch for a child. Others, such as the toy bag or the picture for baby, are somewhat more detailed and challenging.

Cross stitch itself is very easy to learn; there are only a few simple rules, and once you have mastered these, you can attempt any design. As with any craft, practice makes perfect, and you will find that perfection is quickly achieved.

Each cross stitch design is carefully charted and has an accompanying colour key and full instructions for making up the project. Also included is a Basic Skills section, which covers everything from how to prepare your fabric and stretch it in an embroidery hoop or frame, to mounting your cross stitch embroidery over card ready for display.

Whatever your level of skill or interest in the craft, you will enjoy being able to create items from the wide range of projects offered in this book, suitable for children and adults of all ages.

BASIC SKILLS

BEFORE YOU BEGIN

PREPARING THE FABRIC
Even with an average amount of handling, many evenweave fabrics tend to fray at the edges, so it is a good idea to overcast the raw edges, using ordinary sewing thread, before you begin.

THE INSTRUCTIONS
Each project begins with a full list of the materials that you will require; Aida, Tula, Lugana and Linda are all fabrics produced by Zweigart. Note that the measurements given for the embroidery fabric include a minimum of 3cm (1¼in) all around to allow for stretching it in a frame and preparing the edges to prevent them from fraying.

Colour keys for stranded embroidery cottons – DMC, Anchor or Madeira – are given with each chart. It is assumed that you will need to buy one skein of each colour mentioned in a particular key, even though you may use less, but where two or more skeins are needed, this information is included in the main list of requirements.

To work from the charts, particularly those where several symbols are used in close proximity, some readers may find it helpful to have the chart enlarged so that the squares and symbols can be seen more easily. Many photocopying services will do this for a minimum charge.

Before you begin to embroider, always mark the centre of the design with two lines of basting stitches, one vertical and one horizontal, running from edge to edge of the fabric, as indicated by the arrows on the charts.

As you stitch, use the centre lines given on the chart and the basting threads on your fabric as reference points for counting the squares and threads to position your design accurately.

WORKING IN A HOOP
A hoop is the most popular frame for use with small areas of embroidery. It consists of two rings, one fitted inside the other; the outer ring usually has an adjustable screw attachment so that it can be

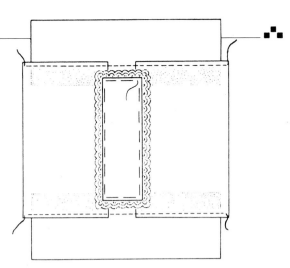

tightened to hold the stretched fabric in place. Hoops are available in several sizes, ranging from 10cm (4in) in diameter to quilting hoops with a diameter of 38cm (15in). Hoops with table stands or floor stands attached are also available.

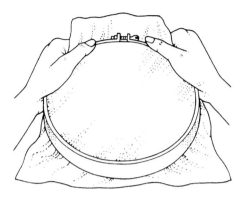

1 To stretch your fabric in a hoop, place the area to be embroidered over the inner ring and press the outer ring over it with the tension screw released. Tissue paper can be placed between the outer ring and the embroidery, so that the hoop does not mark the fabric. Lay the tissue paper over the fabric when you set it in the hoop, then tear away the central, embroidery area.

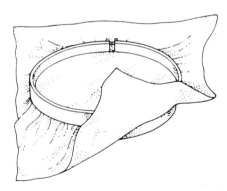

2 Smooth the fabric and, if needed, straighten the grain before tightening the screw. The fabric should be evenly stretched.

EXTENDING EMBROIDERY FABRIC

It is easy to extend a piece of embroidery fabric, such as a bookmark, to stretch it in a hoop.

● Fabric oddments of a similar weight can be used. Simply cut four pieces to size (in other words, to the measurement that will fit both the embroidery fabric and your hoop) and baste them to each side

of the embroidery fabric before stretching it in the hoop in the usual way.

WORKING IN A RECTANGULAR FRAME

Rectangular frames are more suitable for larger pieces of embroidery. They consist of two rollers, with tapes attached, and two flat side pieces, which slot into the rollers and are held in place by pegs or screw attachments. Available in different sizes, either alone or with adjustable table or floor stands, frames are measured by the length of the roller tape, and range in size from 30cm (12in) to 68cm (27in).

As alternatives to a slate frame, canvas stretchers and the backs of old picture frames can be used. Provided there is sufficient extra fabric around the finished size of the embroidery, the edges can be turned under and simply attached with drawing pins (thumb tacks) or staples.

1 To stretch your fabric in a rectangular frame, cut out the fabric, allowing at least an extra 5cm (2in) all around the finished size of the embroidery. Baste a single 12mm (½in) turning on the top and bottom edges and oversew strong tape, 2.5cm (1in) wide, to the other two sides. Mark the centre line both ways with basting stitches. Working from the centre outwards and using strong thread, oversew the top and bottom edges to the roller tapes. Fit the side pieces into the slots, and roll any extra fabric on one roller until the fabric is taut.

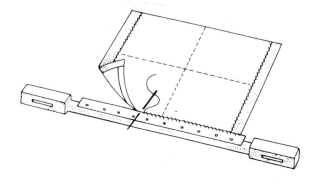

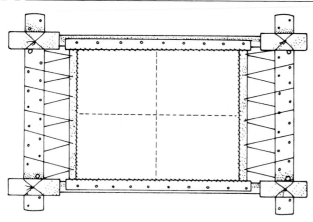

2 Insert the pegs or adjust the screw attachments to secure the frame. Thread a large-eyed needle (chenille needle) with strong thread or fine string and lace both edges, securing the ends around the intersections of the frame. Lace the webbing at 2.5cm (1in) intervals, stretching the fabric evenly.

ENLARGING A GRAPH PATTERN

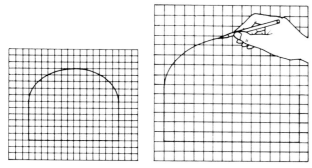

● To enlarge a graph pattern, you will need a sheet of graph paper ruled in 1cm (⅜in) squares, a ruler and pencil. If, for example, the scale is one square to 5cm (2in) you should first mark the appropriate lines to give a grid of the correct size. Copy the graph freehand from the small grid to the larger one, completing one square at a time. Use a ruler to draw the straight lines first, and then copy the freehand curves.

TO BIND AN EDGE

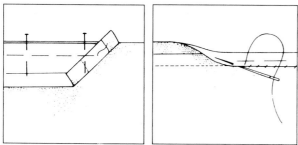

1 Open out the turning on one edge of the bias binding and pin in position on the right side of the fabric, matching the fold to the seamline. Fold over the cut end of the binding. Finish by overlapping the starting point by about 12mm (½in). Baste and machine stitch along the seamline.

2 Fold the binding over the raw edge to the wrong side, baste and, using matching sewing thread, neatly hem to finish.

PIPED SEAMS

Contrasting piping adds a special decorative finish to a seam and looks particularly attractive on items such as cushions and cosies.

You can cover piping cord with either bias-cut fabric of your choice or a bias binding; alternatively, ready-covered piping cord is available in several widths and many colours.

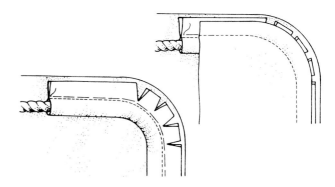

1 To apply piping, pin and baste it to the right side of the fabric, with seam lines matching. Clip into the seam allowance where necessary.

2 With right sides together, place the second piece of fabric on top, enclosing the piping. Baste and then either hand stitch in place or machine stitch, using a zipper foot. Stitch as close to the piping as possible, covering the first line of stitching.

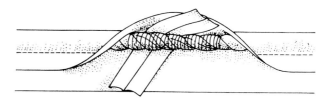

3 To join ends of piping cord together, first overlap the two ends by about 2.5cm (1in). Unpick the two cut ends of bias to reveal the cord. Join the bias strip as shown. Trim and press the seam open. Unravel and splice the two ends of the cord. Fold the bias strip over it, and finish basting around the edge.

MOUNTING EMBROIDERY

The cardboard should be cut to the size of the finished embroidery, with an extra 6mm (¼in) added all around to allow for the recess in the frame.

LIGHTWEIGHT FABRICS

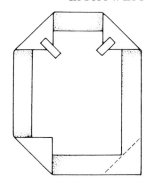 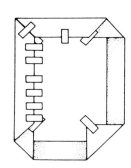

1 Place the emboidery face down, with the cardboard centred on top, and basting and pencil lines matching. Begin by folding over the fabric at each corner and securing it with masking tape.
2 Working first on one side and then the other, fold over the fabric on all sides and secure it firmly with pieces of masking tape, placed about 2.5cm (1in) apart. Also neaten the mitred corners with masking tape, pulling the fabric tightly to give a firm, smooth finish.

HEAVIER FABRICS

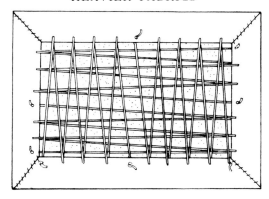

● Lay the embroidery face down, with the cardboard centred on top; fold over the edges of the fabric on opposite sides, making mitred folds at the corners, and lace across, using strong thread. Repeat on the other two sides. Finally, pull up the stitches fairly tightly to stretch the fabric firmly over the cardboard. Overstitch the mitred corners.

CROSS STITCH

For all cross stitch embroidery, the following two methods of working are used. In each case, neat rows of vertical stitches are produced on the back of the fabric.

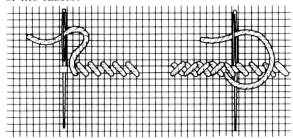

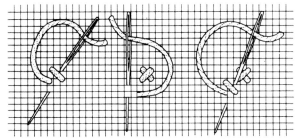

● When stitching large areas, work in horizontal rows. Working from right to left, complete the first row of evenly spaced diagonal stitches over the number of threads specified in the project instructions. Then, working from left to right, repeat the process. Continue in this way, making sure each stitch crosses in the same direction.
● When stitching diagonal lines, work downwards, completing each stitch before moving to the next.

BACKSTITCH

Backstitch is used in the projects to give emphasis to a particular foldline, an outline or a shadow. The stitches are worked over the same number of threads as the cross stitch, forming continuous straight or diagonal lines.

● Make the first stitch from left to right; pass the needle behind the fabric, and bring it out one stitch length ahead to the left. Repeat and continue in this way along the line.

Cards to Treasure

A personalized greetings card containing a small embroidery is a pleasure to make and a way of showing that the recipient is special.

CARDS TO TREASURE

YOU WILL NEED

For each card, measuring 15.5cm × 11cm
(6¼in × 4in):

*19cm × 15cm (7½in × 6in) of white Hardanger
fabric, with 22 threads to 2.5cm (1in)*
*Stranded embroidery cotton in the colours given in
the appropriate panel*
No26 tapestry needle
Double-sided adhesive tape
*Card mount (for suppliers, see page 48),
as appropriate:*
*Christmas Bear card – holly green with round
inner frame, 8cm (3in) in diameter*
*Birthday Bear card – pale blue with round
inner frame, 8cm (3in) in diameter*
*Valentine Bear card – Christmas red with oval
inner frame, 10.5cm × 8cm (4¼in × 3in)*
*Iron-on interfacing (optional – see Making up the
cards) – 12mm larger all-round than the size of
the inner frame of the chosen card*

•

THE EMBROIDERY

All three cards are stitched in the same way and
on the same type of fabric.

Note that it is particularly important with
embroidered cards to avoid excessive overstitching
on the back, as this would cause unsightly lumps
to show through on the right side.

Prepare the fabric, marking the centre lines of
each design with basting stitches, and mount it in
a small hoop, following the instructions on page 5.
Referring to the appropriate chart, complete the
cross stitching, using a single strand in the needle
throughout. Embroider the main areas first, and
then finish with the backstitching. If necessary,
steam press on the wrong side.

It is a good idea to leave the basting stitches in
at this stage, as they will prove useful in helping to
centre your design in the card window.

MAKING UP THE CARDS

It is not strictly necessary to use iron-on interfacing,
but it helps to avoid wrinkles. If you are using interfacing, place it on the back of the embroidery; use a
pencil to mark the basting/registration points on
the interfacing and outer edge of the embroidery.

Remove basting stitches and iron the interfacing in
place, aligning marks.

Trim the embroidery to about 12mm (½in) larger
than the cut-out window, and then, making sure that
the motif is placed in the middle by measuring an
equal distance at each side of the marks, position the
embroidery behind the window. Use double-sided
tape to fix the embroidery into the card, then press
the backing down firmly.

BIRTHDAY ▼		DMC	ANCHOR	MADEIRA
□	White	White	2	White
‖	Medium pink	899	27	0505
x	Deep rose	309	42	0507
c	Delft blue	809	130	0909
	Royal blue*	797	132	0912
I	Light tan	738	942	2013
•	Light brown	434	309	2009
	Very dark coffee*	898	360	2006
■	Black	310	403	Black

Note: black used for bks mouth, very dark coffee* for bear, royal blue* for ribbon.

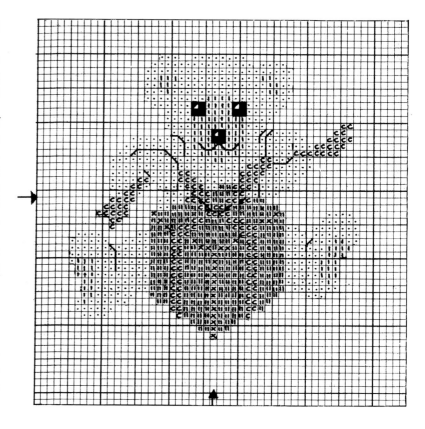

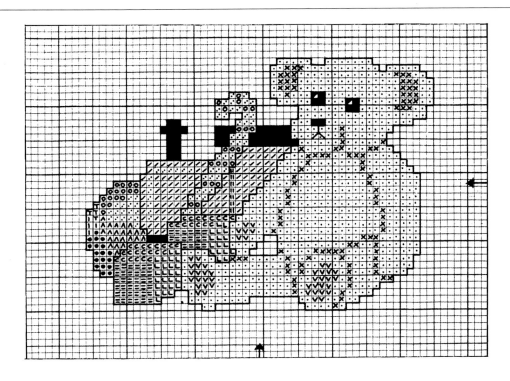

CHRISTMAS ▲		DMC	ANCHOR	MADEIRA
.·	White	White	2	White
c	Pink	3326	26	0504
o	Bright red	666	46	0210
L	Dark lavender	208	110	0804
●	Light pumpkin	970	316	0204
x	Medium tangerine	741	304	0201
·	Dark yellow	743	297	0113
Λ	Medium bright blue	996	433	1103
=	Delft blue	809	130	0909
T	Dark blue	825	162	1011
I	Light emerald	912	209	1212
/	Light green	989	256	1401
II	Dark green	987	245	1403
V	Medium gold brown	976	309	2302
	Very dark grey*	844	401	1810
■	Black	310	403	Black

Note: very dark grey* used for bks outlines, and black for mouth.

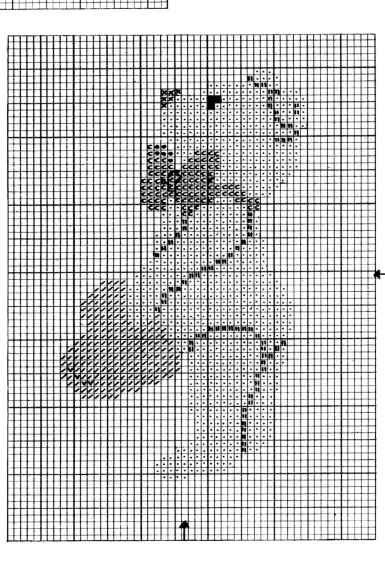

VALENTINE ▶		DMC	ANCHOR	MADEIRA
v	White	White	2	White
/	Red	349	13	0212
c	Medium baby blue	334	161	1003
●	Light navy	312	147	1005
	Medium navy*	311	148	1006
·	Medium old gold	729	907	2209
II	Dark topaz brown	781	308	2213
x	Dark coffee	801	357	2007
■	Black	310	403	Black

Note: medium navy* used for bks ribbon.

Baby's Coverlet

Could any tiny child, or mother, resist the enchantment of these lovely sleepy teddies? This wonderfully soft and practical Afghan fabric, featuring 13cm (5in) squares, is ideal for a baby's coverlet, and easily washable.

BABY'S COVERLET

YOU WILL NEED

For a coverlet, measuring 86cm × 104cm (34in × 41in):

92cm × 110cm (37in × 44in) of
Anne Afghan fabric
Stranded embroidery cotton in the colours given in
the panel; two skeins of tan are required
Matching cream sewing thread
No26 tapestry needle

•

THE EMBROIDERY

Following the diagram, cut the fabric to size. If you are securing the fringe by machine, stitch a zigzag border all around, as indicated. Mark the centre lines of each design with basting stitches, and mount the fabric in a hoop, following the instructions on page 5. Referring to the appropriate chart, complete each design, starting at the centre of each

and using two strands in the needle for cross stitching and one for backstitched lines.

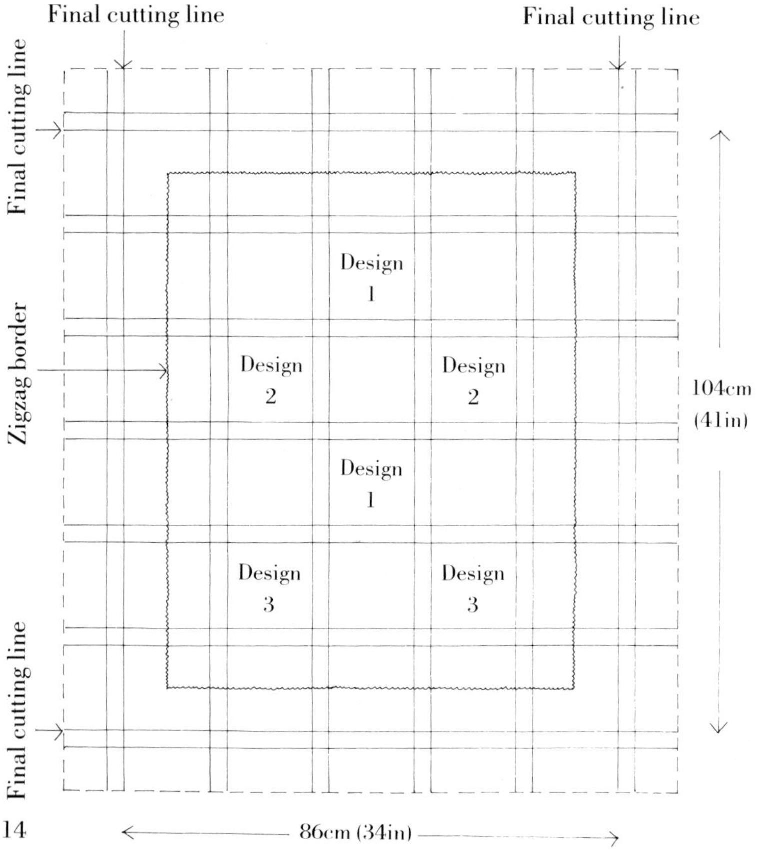

COMPLETING THE COVERLET

Trim the fabric to the final size. To make the fringe, either remove fabric threads one at a time until you reach the zigzag stitch line, or hemstitch, as shown.
Brush out the fringe with a stiff brush.

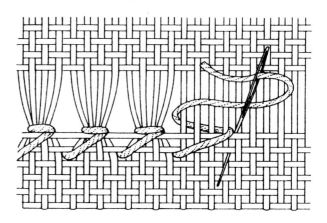

HEMSTITCH

Remove a single thread from the fabric at the hemline (the start of the fringe). Bring the needle out on the right side, two threads below the drawn-thread line. Working from left to right, pick up either two or three threads, as shown in the diagram. Bring the needle out again and insert it behind the fabric, to emerge two threads down, ready to make the next stitch. Before reinserting the needle, pull the thread tight, so that the bound threads form a neat group. To complete the fringe, remove the weft threads below the hemstitching.

Diagram labels (left figure):

Final cutting line — Final cutting line

Final cutting line

Zigzag border

Design 1

Design 2 — Design 2

Design 1

Design 3 — Design 3

Final cutting line

104cm (41in)

86cm (34in)

BABY'S COVERLET ▶		DMC	ANCHOR	MADEIRA
L	White	White	2	White
·•	Medium lavender	210	108	0802
●	Dark carnation	891	29	0411
I	Delft blue	809	130	0909
X	Light emerald	912	209	1212
∕	Very light yellow	3078	292	0102
O	Light topaz	727	293	0110
C	Very light brown	435	365	2010
V	Light brown	434	309	2009
•	Tan	436	363	2011
∧	Light grey	415	398	1803
	Steel grey*	317	400	1714
	Dark steel grey*	413	401	1713
	Black*	310	403	Black

Note: black used for bks clock hands, clock numbers steel grey*, all outlines dark steel grey*.*

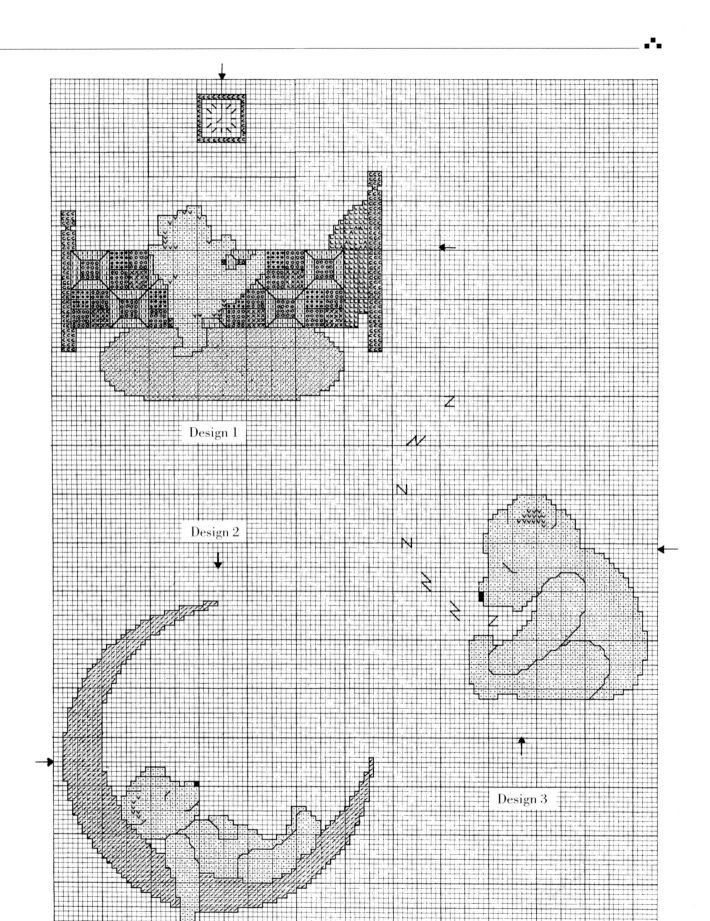

Design 1

Design 2

Design 3

15

Porcelain Trinket Boxes

These beautiful porcelain trinket boxes make gifts which are both useful and decorative. They can adorn a dressing table, an occasional table, or even a mantelpiece.

PORCELAIN
TRINKET BOXES

YOU WILL NEED

For each box:

*15cm (6in) square of white Hardanger fabric, with
22 threads to 2.5cm (1in)
Stranded embroidery cotton in the colours given in
the appropriate panel
No26 tapestry needle
Trinket box (for suppliers, see page 48):
for Standing Bear, an oval box, measuring
8.5cm × 6cm (3¼in × 2¼in); for Heart Bear,
a heart-shaped box, measuring 7cm × 8cm
(2¾in × 3in); for Marching Bear, a circular box,
measuring 8cm (3in) in diameter*

•

THE EMBROIDERY

All three designs are stitched in the same way and
on the same type of fabric. If you wish to embroider
all of the designs, you may be able to economize
on fabric by using one large piece, remembering to
allow sufficient space between each picture.

Prepare the fabric, marking the centre lines of
the design with basting stitches, and mount it in a
small hoop, following the instructions on page 5.
Referring to the appropriate chart, and starting at
the centre, complete the cross stitching, using a
single strand in the needle throughout. Embroider
the main areas first, and then finish with the backstitching. If necessary, steam press on the wrong
side.

It is a good idea to leave the basting stitches in
at this stage, as they will prove useful in helping to
centre your design in the lid.

ASSEMBLING THE LID

Place the finished embroidery face up on a firm, flat
surface. Gently remove all parts from the lid of
the trinket box. Use the rim of the lid and the
basting stitches to centre the design. Using a hard
pencil, draw a line on the fabric, around the outer
edge of the lid, then cut along the drawn line.
Remove basting stitches.

To assemble the lid, replace the clear acetate and
place your design in the lid, with the right side to the

acetate. Place the sponge behind your design. Push
the metal locking disc very firmly into place using
thumb pressure, with the raised side of the disc
facing the sponge. When the locking disc is tightly in
position, use a little glue to secure the flock lining
card to it.

STANDING BEAR ▼		DMC	ANCHOR	MADEIRA
I	Medium delft blue	799	140	0910
•	Christmas gold	783	307	2211
x	Dark topaz	781	308	2213
o	Dark mahogany	400	351	2305
	Dark beaver grey*	844	401	1810
■	Black	310	403	Black

Note: black used for bks mouth, dark beaver grey for outlines.*

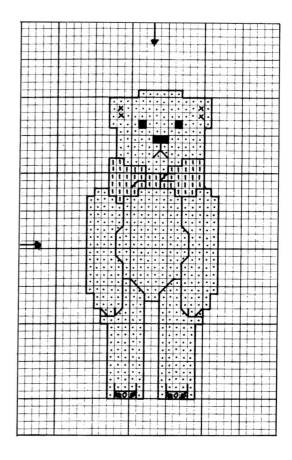

ALTERNATIVE USES

These designs are very simple and easy to stitch, and would make ideal first projects for a child who is interested in embroidery.

Rather than working on the rather fine fabric specified for the trinket boxes, however, it might be preferable to start on a fabric with a larger weave, say with 14 threads per 2.5cm (1in). In this case, the finished designs would, of course, be considerably larger and could not be used for the trinket box lids. Instead, the designs could perhaps be used for greetings cards (see page 8), or set in picture frames (see page 28).

Another way of using these designs would be to embroider them on preserve pot covers (ready made covers, trimmed with lace, can be purchased from specialist suppliers, see page 48).

To work out how much fabric you will need if you are changing the scale, count the number of stitches of your chosen design each way. Divide these numbers by the number of threads or blocks per 2.5cm (1in) of your fabric, then add an appropriate margin around the basic design size.

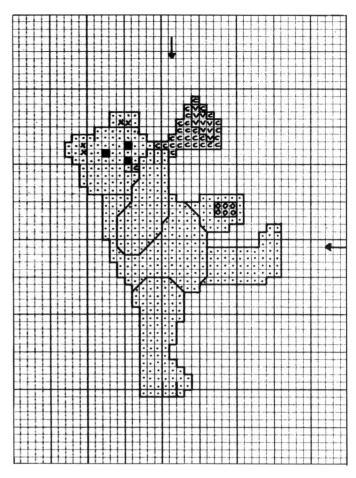

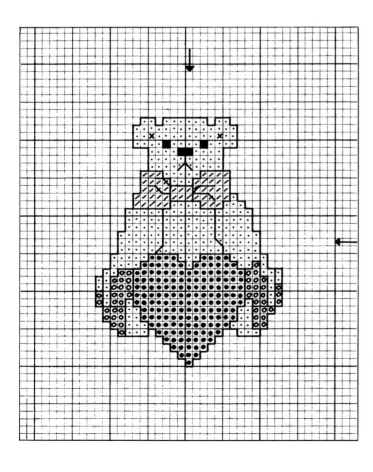

MARCHING BEAR ▲	DMC	ANCHOR	MADEIRA
• Christmas gold	783	307	2211
v Deep canary	972	303	0107
c Dark yellow	743	297	0113
x Dark topaz	781	308	2213
o Dark mahogany	400	351	2305
Dark beaver grey*	844	401	1810
■ Black	310	403	Black

Note: black used for bks mouth, dark beaver grey* for outlines.

HEART BEAR ◄	DMC	ANCHOR	MADEIRA
• Bright red	666	46	0210
• Christmas gold	783	307	2211
╱ Dark green	701	227	1305
x Dark topaz	781	308	2213
o Dark mahogany	400	351	2305
Dark beaver grey*	844	401	1810
■ Black	310	403	Black

Note: black used for bks mouth, dark beaver grey* for outlines.

Lace-edged Cushions

These beautiful lace-edged cushions with their cheerful, friendly bears are simple to make and will brighten up any child's room, either scattered on the bed or on a favourite chair.

LACE-EDGED CUSHIONS

YOU WILL NEED

For each cushion, measuring 25cm (10in) square,
excluding lace edging:

*35cm (14in) square of white Aida fabric, with
14 threads to 2.5cm (1in)*
*27.5cm (11in) square of contrast fabric, to back
your cushion*
*2.4m (2²⁄₃yds) of white lace edging,
4cm (1¹⁄₂in) deep*
*Stranded embroidery cotton in the colours given
in the appropriate panel*
Matching sewing thread
No24 tapestry needle
27.5cm (11in) square cushion pad

THE EMBROIDERY

Prepare the fabric, marking the centre lines of the
design with basting stitches, and mount it in a hoop
or frame, following the instructions on page 5.
Referring to the appropriate chart, complete the
cross stitching, starting at the centre and using two
strands in the needle throughout. Embroider the
main areas first, and then finish with the backstitching, this time using a single strand in a
needle. Steam press on the wrong side.

MAKING UP THE COVER

Trim the embroidery to measure 27.5cm (11in)
square. Using a tiny french seam, join the short
edges of the lace together. Run a gathering thread
close to the straight edge; pull up the gathers to fit
and, with the right side of the embroidery facing and
the lace lying on the fabric, baste the edging to the

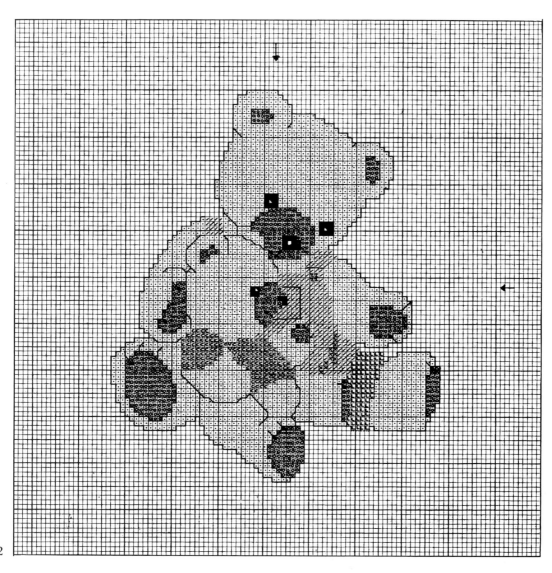

outer edge, placing it just inside the 12mm (½in) seam allowance. Adjust the gathers evenly, allowing a little extra fullness at the corners. Machine stitch the frill in place.

With right sides together, place the backing fabric on top; baste and machine stitch around, leaving a 20cm (8in) opening in the middle of one side. Remove basting stitches; trim across the corners, and turn the cover through. Insert the cushion pad and slipstitch the opening to secure it.

FATHER AND SON ◄	DMC	ANCHOR	MADEIRA
□ White	White	2	White
C Christmas red	321	47	0510
V Garnet red	815	43	0513
L Baby blue	3325	159	1002
X Medium navy	311	148	1006
∕ Dark baby blue	322	978	1004
O Pale golden wheat	3047	886	2205
Z Medium topaz	782	307	2212
• Tan	436	363	2011
Dark coffee*	801	357	2007*
■ Black	310	403	Black

Note: dark coffee* used for bks outline bodies, dark baby blue for trouser leg, medium navy for other clothing.

MOTHER AND DAUGHTER ▼	DMC	ANCHOR	MADEIRA
□ White	White	2	White
∕ Pink	3326	26	0504
• Dark pink	335	42	0506
C Medium lavender	210	108	0802
‖ Dark lavender	208	110	0804
O Pale golden wheat	3047	886	2205
• Tan	436	363	2011
Dark coffee*	801	357	2007*
Light grey*	415	398	1803
■ Black	310	403	Black

Note: dark coffee* used for bks outline bodies, light grey* for sleeve.

Christmas Stocking

A hand-embroidered stocking is a present that will delight a small child and can become a treasured part of the Christmas tradition. This small, pretty stocking is just the right size to hold sweets and tiny toys, or even a small teddy.

CHRISTMAS STOCKING

For the Christmas stocking, measuring
25cm × 18cm (10in × 7¼in) overall:

*Two 30cm (12in) squares of navy Aida fabric, with
14 threads to 2.5cm (1in)
1.1m (1¼yd) of red bias binding
Stranded embroidery cotton in the colours given
in the panel
Metallic threads in gold and silver
Two 30cm (12in) squares of lightweight synthetic
batting (optional)
Two 30cm (12in) squares of lining fabric, in navy
or a contrast colour (optional)
Matching red sewing thread
No24 tapestry needle*

*NOTE The stocking seen here is unlined, but if you
wish to make a lined and padded version, for
greater durability – and to help to conceal the
shapes of the contents – you will require the
optional batting and lining listed above.*

•

THE EMBROIDERY

Prepare the fabric, marking the centre lines of
the design with basting stitches, and mount it in a
hoop or frame, following the instructions on page 5.
Referring to the chart, complete the cross stitching,
starting at the centre and using three strands in the
needle when working with stranded cotton and two
strands when using the metallic thread. Embroider
the main areas first, and then finish with the backstitching, using two strands of cotton in the needle.
Remove basting stitches and, if necessary, steam
press on the wrong side.

MAKING UP THE STOCKING

Trace the template for the stocking outline on tracing
paper, marking the position of the arrows. It is not
necessary to cut out the shape at this stage, simply
pin the tracing paper to the embroidery fabric,
making sure that the embroidery falls in the correct
position, or use strips of masking tape to hold it in
place. Cut out the shape, then cut out a mirror image
shape from the fabric that is not embroidered.

If you wish to make a hanging loop for the stocking, take a short length of binding – approximately

5cm (2in). Bring the folded edges together and slipstitch. Set the strip to one side.

Place the two pieces of fabric with wrong sides
together and baste. Taking a 12mm (½in) seam
allowance, machine around the stocking, leaving the
top edge open. Trim the seam neatly to 6mm (¼in)
from the stitching line. Remove the basting stitches.

Bind around the trimmed seam to neaten it. You
can either follow the instructions given on page 6 or
simply place the binding over the edge, and machine
stitch through all layers, close to the folded edge. If
you are adding a hanging loop, take the prepared
strip of binding and fold it in two. Position the loop at
the top of the back seam of the stocking, with the raw
edges level with the raw edge of the stocking top.
Bind around the top of the stocking, catching the
loop in with the binding.

LINED VERSION

If you are making a padded and lined version, use
the template to cut out a pair of shapes each from the
batting and lining fabrics. Before making up the
stocking as described above, place a fabric, batting
and lining shape together, with the batting in the
middle of the sandwich and the lining and fabric
layers right side outwards. Pin and baste together.
Repeat for the other half of the stocking, then pro-
ceed to make up the stocking as described above,
but trim the batting right back to the seamline before
adding the binding.

CHRISTMAS STOCKING ▶	DMC	ANCHOR	MADEIRA
∴ White	White	2	White
o Medium violet	553	98	0712
‖ Christmas red	321	47	0510
● Garnet red	815	43	0513
· Pale golden wheat	3047	886	2205
c Bright canary	973	297	0105
v Kelly green	702	226	1306
∕ Tan	436	363	2011
∧ Medium brown	433	371	2008
■ Black	310	403	Black
H Silver thread			
= Gold thread			

Note: black used for bks mouth.

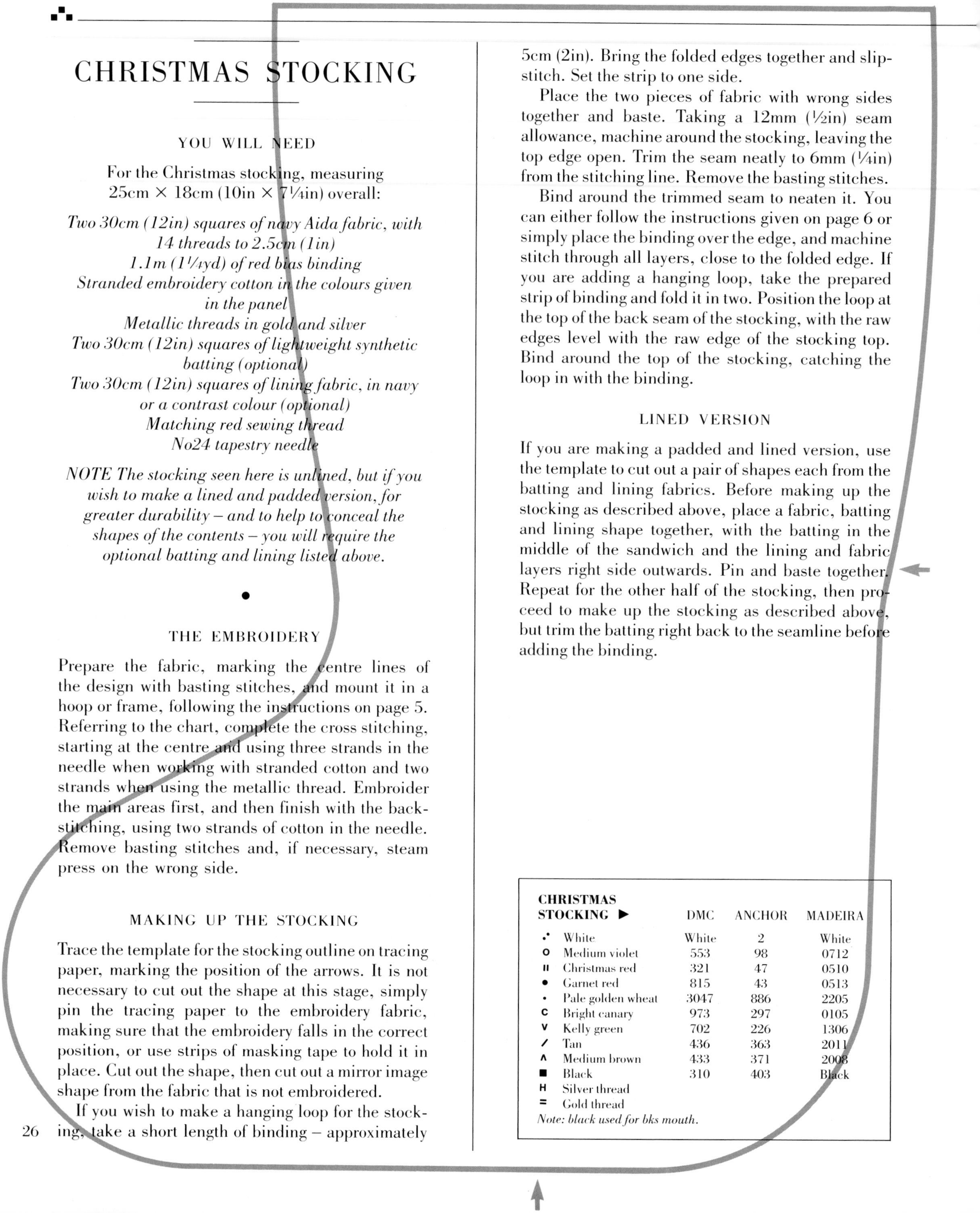

Teddy Pictures

These delightful miniature pictures
will make an attractive addition
to your home, whether displayed
singly or together.
Either of the designs would make a
lovely gift to welcome a new baby.

TEDDY PICTURES

YOU WILL NEED

For the Balloon Bear picture, measuring
18cm × 13cm (7¼in × 5in), framed:

*23cm (9in) square of Ainring Aida fabric in ecru,
with 18 threads to 2.5cm (1in)
Stranded embroidery cotton in the colours given in
the appropriate panel
No26 tapestry needle
Oval brass frame (for suppliers, see page 48)*

For the Reading Bears picture, measuring 15cm
(6in) in diameter, framed:

*23cm (9in) square of Ainring Aida fabric in ecru,
with 18 threads to 2.5cm (1in)
Stranded embroidery cotton in the colours given in
the appropriate panel
No26 tapestry needle
Round brass frame (for suppliers, see page 48)*

•

THE EMBROIDERY

Both designs are stitched in the same way and on
the same type of fabric. If you wish to embroider
them both, you may be able to economize on fabric
by using one large piece, remembering to allow
sufficient space between the pictures.

Prepare the fabric, marking the centre lines of
(each) design with basting stitches, and mount it in
a hoop, following the instructions on page 5. Referring to the appropriate chart, complete the cross
stitching, starting at the centre and using two
strands in the needle throughout. Embroider the
main areas first, and then finish with the backstitching, this time using one strand of thread in the
needle. Steam press on the wrong side.

It is a good idea to leave the basting stitches in
at this stage, as they will prove useful in helping to
centre your design in the frame.

FRAMING A PICTURE

Each picture is framed in the same way. Gently
remove all parts of the frame. Place the card template over the chart and mark the centre both ways,
using a soft pencil. Lay the embroidery face down
with the card on top, matching basting stitches and
lines, and draw around the card with a pencil.

Working freehand, draw a second line about 4cm
(1½in) outside, and cut along this outer line.

With double sewing thread in the needle, make a
line of running stitches about 2cm (¾in) in from the
raw edge, close to the marked line. Place the card on
the wrong side and pull up the thread, spacing the
gathers evenly, and making sure the fabric grain is
straight. Secure the thread firmly. Add pieces of
masking tape over the edges of the fabric for extra
strength. Finish the assembly, following the manufacturer's instructions.

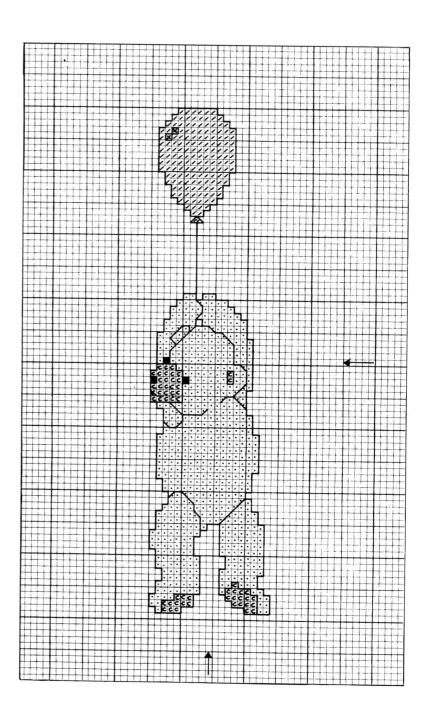

READING BEARS ▲		DMC	ANCHOR	MADEIRA
□	White	White	2	White
•	Dark peach	351	10	0214
╱	Topaz	725	306	0108
L	Light old gold	676	891	2208
o	Dark old gold	680	901	2210
∙	Medium blue	826	161	1012
‖	Very light brown	435	365	2010
●	Medium brown	433	371	2008
	Very dark beaver*	844	401	1810
■	Black	310	403	Black

Note: black used for bks eyes, other outlines very dark beaver.*

BALLOON BEAR ◄		DMC	ANCHOR	MADEIRA
x	White	White	2	White
╱	Medium blue	826	161	1012
c	Very light tan	738	942	2013
•	Light brown	434	309	2009
	Very dark beaver*	844	401	1810
■	Black	310	403	Black

Note: very dark beaver used for bks outlines.*

Toy Bag

Suitable for a child of any age group, this toy bag will make an extremely practical gift, and a bright and attractive feature in the playroom or nursery. The bag has a draw-string top and is both large enough and strong enough to hold many small toys.

TOY BAG

YOU WILL NEED

For a toy bag, measuring 60cm × 44cm
(24in × 17½in):

65cm (26in) of cream pearl Aida fabric, 110cm
(43in) wide, with 11 threads to 2.5cm (1in)
65cm (26in) of firm, unbleached cotton (calico),
110cm (43in) wide, for the lining
250cm (2½yds) of white cord, 6mm (¼in)
in diameter
Stranded embroidery cotton in the colours
given in the panel
Matching sewing thread
No24 tapestry needle

•

THE EMBROIDERY

Take a piece of fabric measuring 65cm × 50cm
(26in × 20in). Prepare the fabric, marking the
centre lines of the design with basting stitches;
ensure that there is a clearance around the design
area of 15.5cm (6½in) at the sides and bottom, and
26cm (10¼in) at the top, and mount it in a hoop
or frame, following the instructions on page 5.
Referring to the chart, complete the cross stitching,
using three strands in the needle throughout.
Embroider the main areas first, and then finish with
the backstitching, this time using two strands of
thread in the needle. If necessary, steam press on
the wrong side.

MAKING THE BAG

Trim the edges of the embroidered fabric until the
piece measures 47cm × 63.5cm (18½in × 25in),
with a clearance around the design of 14cm (5½in)
at the sides and bottom and 25.5cm (10in) from the
top. Cut a second piece of Aida fabric to match.

    With right sides together and taking a 12mm
(½in) seam allowance, stitch the side seams,
stitching down from the top for 5cm (2in), leaving
a gap of 3.5cm (1¼in), and then continuing to the
bottom (A).

    Join the bottom seam. Press the seams flat and
topstitch around each gap, 6mm (¼in) from the
pressed edge, as shown (B).

    Cut two lining pieces, each measuring 47cm ×
62.5cm (18½in × 24½in). Place the two pieces of
lining fabric with right sides together and stitch the

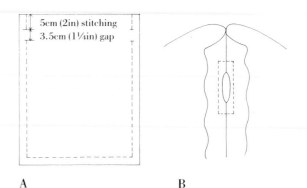

A   B

side seams (all the way), and then the bottom seam,
leaving an opening of 15cm (6in) for turning (C).

    Place the outer bag into the lining, with right sides
together, and stitch around the top edge. Press
seams flat, then turn the bag right side out through
the opening. Slipstitch the opening to close it. Press
around the top of the bag, then topstitch two lines,
6mm (¼in) above and below the side openings (D).
Thread the cord twice through the resulting case-
ment and tie the ends together.

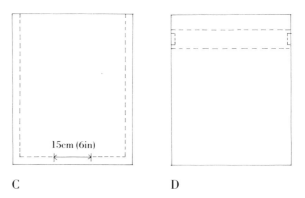

C   D

TOY BAG ▶		DMC	ANCHOR	MADEIRA
□	White	White	2	White
V	Garnet	816	20	0512
ᴸ	Dark Christmas red	498	47	0511
−	Lemon yellow	307	289	0104
T	Christmas gold	783	307	2211
\	Tangerine	740	316	0202
/	Bright orange	606	335	0209
ᴧ	Baby blue	3325	159	1002
=	Medium baby blue	334	161	1003
C	Dark baby blue	322	978	1004
X	Aquamarine	992	187	1202
●	Royal blue	797	132	0912
H	Medium navy	311	148	1006
‖	Dark emerald	910	228	1310
O	Very light tan	738	942	2013
˙•	Tan	436	363	2011
•	Medium topaz	782	307	2212
Z	Light brown	434	309	2009
L	Dark coffee	801	357	2007
	Very dark beaver*	844	401	1810
■	Black	310	403	Black

Note: very dark beaver* used for all bks outlines.

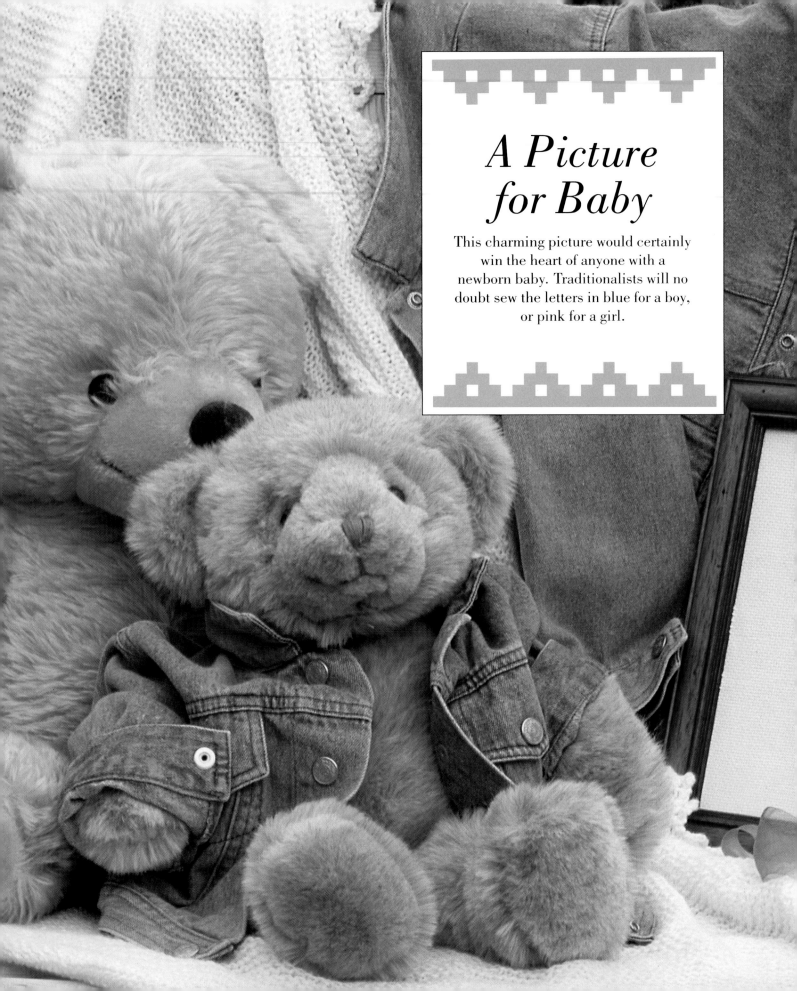

A Picture for Baby

This charming picture would certainly win the heart of anyone with a newborn baby. Traditionalists will no doubt sew the letters in blue for a boy, or pink for a girl.

A PICTURE FOR BABY

YOU WILL NEED

For the picture, measuring 50cm × 24cm
(20in × 9½in), unframed:

*58.5cm × 31.5cm (23in × 12½in) of white Aida
fabric, with 14 threads to 2.5cm (1in)
Stranded embroidery cotton in the colours given
in the panel; two skeins of tan are required, and
three of either baby blue or pale dusty rose
50cm × 24cm (20in × 9½in) of firm cardboard,
for a mount
50cm × 24cm (20in × 9½in) of iron-on
interfacing (optional – see Mounting the picture)
No24 tapestry needle
Picture frame of your choice*

THE EMBROIDERY

Prepare the fabric, marking the centre lines of the
design with basting stitches, and mount it in a
frame, following the instructions on page 5. Referring to the chart, complete the cross stitching,
using three strands in the needle throughout.
Embroider the main areas first, and then finish with
the backstitching, this time using two strands of
thread in the needle. If necessary, steam press on
the wrong side.

It is a good idea to leave the basting stitches in
at this stage, as they will prove useful in helping to
centre your design on the mount.

MOUNTING THE PICTURE

Take care that your working surface is absolutely
clean and dry. If you wish to use an iron-on interfacing, to help to avoid wrinkles, iron this to the back
of the embroidery, following the same procedure as
for the cards on page 10. If you are not using interfacing, leave the basting stitches in place and
remove them after mounting.

Mount your picture on the firm cardboard, following the instructions given for heavier fabrics. Mark
the centre of the board at the top, bottom and sides,
and match centre marks for accurate alignment.

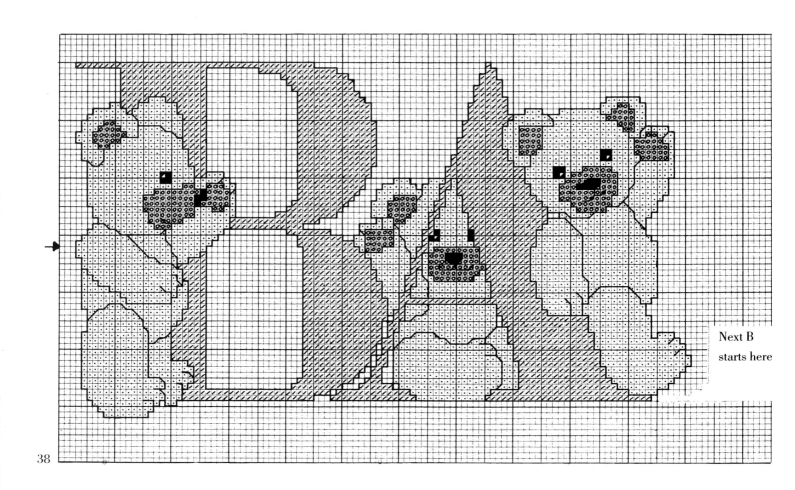

Next B
starts here

PICTURE FOR BABY	DMC	ANCHOR	MADEIRA
△ White	White	2	White
⟋ Baby blue	3325	159	1002
Dark baby blue*	322	978	1004
⟋ Pale dusty rose	963	48	0608
Dark dusty rose*	961	40	0610
o Pale golden wheat	3047	886	2205
· Tan	436	363	2011
Medium brown*	433	371	2008
■ Black	310	403	Black

Note: outline pale golden wheat with medium brown, baby blue
with dark baby blue* or pale dusty rose with dark dusty rose*;
use either baby blues (for a boy) or dusty pinks (for a girl); two
skeins needed of tan, and three of either baby blue or pale
dusty rose.*

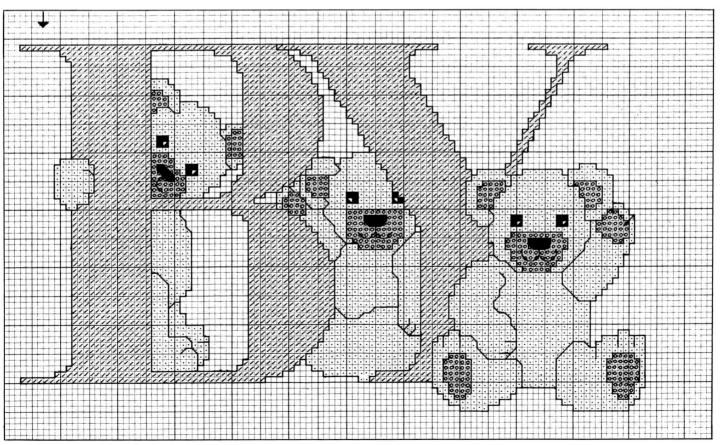

Decorative Motifs

Even the plainest of children's clothes can be turned into something rather special with the addition of these small, attractive motifs.

DECORATIVE MOTIFS

YOU WILL NEED

To embroider either of these decorations on your chosen item of children's clothing:

Zweigart's waste canvas (for suppliers, see page 48), with 14 threads per 2.5cm (1in), as below – for Kite Bear, 23cm × 18cm (9in × 7¼in); for Bears and Hearts, a strip of canvas 10cm (4in) deep and the desired length of the border Stranded embroidery cotton in the colours given in the appropriate panel No24 tapestry needle Fine tweezers Water spray bottle

•

THE EMBROIDERY

To ensure that your finished embroidery lies straight on the garment, align the blue threads horizontally or vertically, either with the weave of the fabric or with the seams of the garment, whichever is appropriate. Pin the canvas centrally over the area where the design is to be stitched, and baste it in place around the edges. Remove the pins.

Treat each pair of canvas threads as a single thread, and stitch the design as you would on any other evenweave fabric. Start stitching at the top of the design and work downwards, using two strands for the cross stitch, and one for the backstitch.

You can start and finish threads as usual, by anchoring with your first few stitches, and threading the ends of the threads in on the back of the work when you finish. If the garments are going to be laundered frequently, you may want to begin and end threads with a small knot for added security.

When you have completed your cross stitch embroidery, cut away the extra canvas, leaving approximately 12mm (½in) all around the design. Dampen the right side with slightly warm water (do not soak it) and leave it for a few minutes until the sizing softens. Use tweezers to pull each of the canvas threads out one at a time. Moisten again if required. Resist the temptation to pull out more than one thread at a time, as you may damage your embroidery.

As if by magic, you are now left with the finished design on your garment. Place your embroidered garment wrong side up over a dry towel and press, being careful not to flatten the stitches.

If you choose to sew your design onto fabric which is dry-cleanable only, the canvas threads can be softened by rubbing them together (taking care not to damage the embroidery). It should then be possible to remove the threads one by one without having to use water.

BEARS AND HEARTS ▼		DMC	ANCHOR	MADEIRA
•	Deep rose	309	42	0507
╱	Christmas gold	783	307	2211
■	Black	310	403	Black

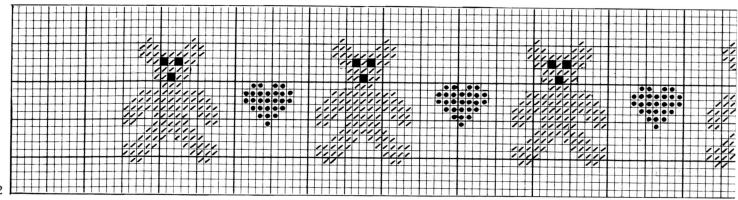

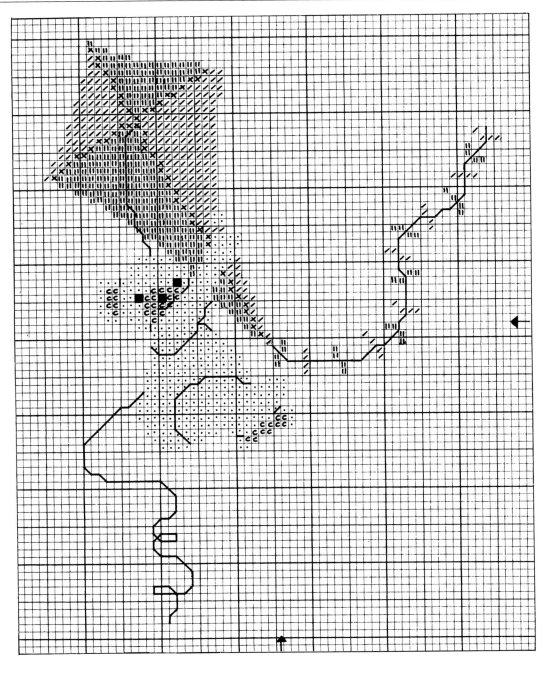

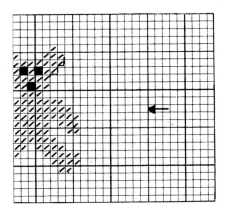

KITE BEAR ▲		DMC	ANCHOR	MADEIRA
∕	Pink	3326	26	0504
ıı	Delft blue	809	130	0909
c	Pale old gold	677	886	2207
x	Light old gold	676	891	2208
•	Medium beige	3032	888	2104
	Grey brown*	3022	8581	1903
	Dark grey brown*	3021	382	1904
■	Black	310	403	Black

Note: use dark grey brown* for bks outline of bear and dark grey brown* for kite.

Dressing-Table Set

What little girl could resist the charm of this silver-plated set of hairbrush and mirror? Two complementary designs make this a delightful gift for a teddy fan.

DRESSING-TABLE SET

No26 tapestry needle
Dressing-table set (for suppliers, see page 48)

●

YOU WILL NEED

For the dressing-table set – handmirror with back, measuring 13cm × 11.5cm (5in × 4½in), hairbrush with back, measuring 10cm × 9cm (4in × 3½in):

44cm × 22cm (17½in × 8½in) of white Hardanger fabric, with 22 threads to 2.5cm (1in)
Iron-on interfacing (optional) – two pieces, one measuring 14cm × 13cm (5½in × 5in) and one 11cm × 10cm (4¼in × 4in)
Stranded embroidery cotton in the colours given in the appropriate panels

THE EMBROIDERY

Both designs are stitched in the same way and on the same type of fabric. You may be able to economize on fabric by using one large piece, remembering to allow sufficient space between the pictures.

Prepare the fabric, marking the centre lines of each design with basting stitches, and mount it in a hoop or frame, following the instructions on page 5. Referring to the appropriate chart and starting at the centre, complete the cross stitching, using one strand in the needle throughout. Embroider the main areas first, and then finish with the backstitching. Steam press on the wrong side.

BUTTERFLY BEAR ▶	DMC	ANCHOR	MADEIRA
□ White	White	2	White
╱ Medium violet	553	98	0712
c Dark violet	550	101	0714
• Christmas gold	783	307	2211
‖ Dark topaz	780	309	2214
● Dark coffee	801	357	2007
x Dark beaver	645	400	1811
■ Black	310	403	Black

Note: dark beaver also used for bks.

It is a good idea to leave the basting stitches in at this stage, as they will prove useful in helping to centre your design in the frame.

ASSEMBLING THE DRESSING-TABLE SET

If you prefer to use iron-on interfacing to avoid wrinkles, first iron a piece of the appropriate size to the back of each embroidery, transferring the registration marks as described for the cards on page 10. If you are not using interfacing, leave the basting stitches in at this stage.

The paper templates supplied by the manufacturers may vary in size so, in order to get an exact fit for each piece, cut out the embroidery, using the template supplied with each piece, but first mark the centre on the template both ways in pencil. In each case, place the template with the marked side on the wrong side of the embroidery; match the pencil lines to the basting stitches, and draw around with a soft pencil. This will help you to centre your embroidery.

Before cutting out, place the template inside the particular frame and check to see how much more fabric, if any, should be included beyond the pencil line. This is a critical stage in the assembly, because the return on the frames is very shallow and therefore does not allow for adjustment if the fabric has been cut too small.

When you are satisfied, cut out the fabric and remove any remaining basting stitches.

Complete the assembly of both pieces, following the manufacturer's instructions.

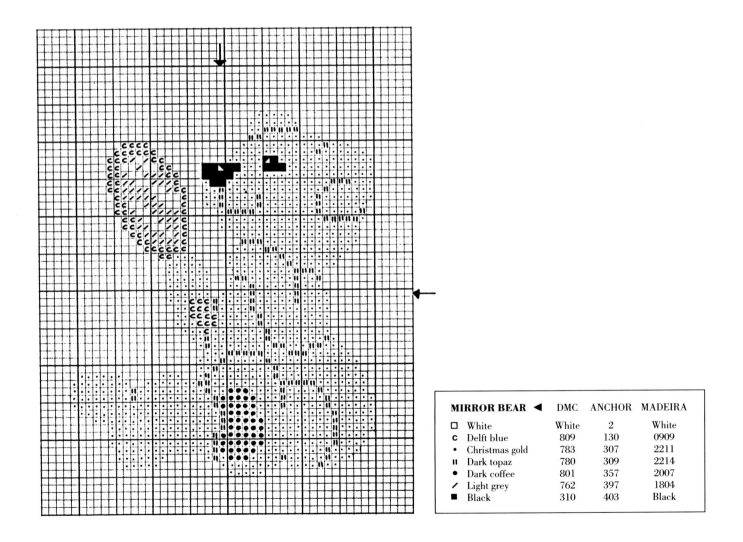

MIRROR BEAR ◄	DMC	ANCHOR	MADEIRA
□ White	White	2	White
c Delft blue	809	130	0909
• Christmas gold	783	307	2211
ıı Dark topaz	780	309	2214
● Dark coffee	801	357	2007
∕ Light grey	762	397	1804
■ Black	310	403	Black

ACKNOWLEDGEMENTS

The author would like to thank the following people for their help with this book.

For the embroidery work – Odette Robinson, Allison Mortley, Linda Potter, Barbara Hodgkinson, Jenny Whitlock, Libby Shaw, Lesley Buckerfield and Dawn Parmley.
For making up the projects – Louise Wells.

Thanks are also due to DMC Creative World Ltd, for supplying fabrics, threads and card mounts, and to Framecraft Miniatures Limited, for supplying brass frames, porcelain trinket boxes, and the dressing-table set. Both suppliers request that a stamped, self-addressed envelope be enclosed with all enquiries.

SUPPLIERS

The following mail order company has supplied some of the basic items needed for making up the projects in this book:

Framecraft Miniatures Ltd
372/376 Summer Lane
Hockley
Birmingham, B19 3QA
England
Telephone: 0121 212 4442

Addresses for Framecraft stockists worldwide
Ireland Needlecraft Pty Ltd
PO Box 1175
Narre Warren MDC
Victoria 3805
Australia

Danish Art Needlework
PO Box 442, Lethbridge
Alberta T1J 3Z1
Canada

Sanyei Imports
PO Box 5, Hashima Shi
Gifu 501-62
Japan

The Embroidery Shop
286 Queen Street
Masterton
New Zealand

Anne Brinkley Designs Inc.
246 Walnut Street
Newton
Mass. 02160
USA

S A Threads and Cottons Ltd
43 Somerset Road
Cape Town
South Africa

For information on your nearest stockist of embroidery cotton, contact the following:

DMC
(also distributors of Zweigart fabrics)

UK
DMC Creative World Ltd
62 Pullman Road, Wigston
Leicester, LE8 2DY
Telephone: 0116 2811040

USA
The DMC Corporation
Port Kearney, Building 10
South Kearney
N.J. 07302
Telephone: 201 589 0606

AUSTRALIA
DMC (Australia) Pty Ltd
PO Box 317
Earlwood
NSW 2206
Telephone: 02 9559 3088

COATS AND ANCHOR

UK
Coats Paton Crafts
McMullen Road
Darlington
Co. Durham DL1 1YQ
Telephone: 01325 365457

USA
Coats & Clark
PO Box 24998
Dept CO1
Greenville SC 29616
Telephone: 800 243 0810

AUSTRALIA
Coats Spencer Crafts
Level 1, 382 Wellington Road
Mulgrave
Victoria 3170
Telephone: 03 9561 2288

MADEIRA

UK
Madeira Threads (UK) Ltd
Thirsk Industrial Park
York Road, Thirsk
N. Yorkshire, YO7 3BX
Telephone: 01845 524880

USA
Madeira Marketing Ltd
600 East 9th Street
Michigan City
IN 46360
Telephone: 219 873 1000

AUSTRALIA
Penguin Threads Pty Ltd
25-27 Izett Street
Prahran
Victoria 3181
Telephone: 039529 4400